Hughes

by Iain Gray

Lang Syne
PUBLISHING
WRITING *to* REMEMBER

WRITING *to* REMEMBER

79 Main Street, Newtongrange,
Midlothian EH22 4NA
Tel: 0131 344 0414   Fax: 0845 075 6085
E-mail: info@lang-syne.co.uk
www.langsyneshop.co.uk

Design by Dorothy Meikle
Printed by Printwell Ltd
© Lang Syne Publishers Ltd 2016

ISBN 978-1-85217-588-7

Hughes

MOTTO:
Kymmer-yn Lydeirnon
(the name of the lordship of the family).

CREST:
A black lion emerging from a crown.

NAME variations include:
Hews
Hues
Huse

Chapter one:

The origins of popular surnames

by George Forbes and Iain Gray

If you don't know where you came from, you won't know where you're going is a frequently quoted observation and one that has a particular resonance today when there has been a marked upsurge in interest in genealogy, with increasing numbers of people curious to trace their family roots.

Main sources for genealogical research include census returns and official records of births, marriages and deaths – and the key to unlocking the detail they contain is obviously a family surname, one that has been 'inherited' and passed from generation to generation.

No matter our station in life, we all have a surname – but it was not until about the middle of the fourteenth century that the practice of being identified by a particular surname became commonly established throughout the British Isles.

Previous to this, it was normal for a person to be identified through the use of only a forename.

But as population gradually increased and there were many more people with the same forename, surnames were adopted to distinguish one person, or community, from another.

Many common English surnames are patronymic in origin, meaning they stem from the forename of one's father – with 'Johnson,' for example, indicating 'son of John.'

It was the Normans, in the wake of their eleventh century conquest of Anglo-Saxon England, a pivotal moment in the nation's history, who first brought surnames into usage – although it was a gradual process.

For the Normans, these were names initially based on the title of their estates, local villages and chateaux in France to distinguish and identify these landholdings.

Such grand descriptions also helped enhance the prestige of these warlords and generally glorify their lofty positions high above the humble serfs slaving away below in the pecking order who had only single names, often with Biblical connotations as in Pierre and Jacques.

The only descriptive distinctions among the peasantry concerned their occupations, like 'Pierre the swineherd' or 'Jacques the ferryman.'

Roots of surnames that came into usage in England not only included Norman-French, but also Old French, Old Norse, Old English, Middle English, German, Latin, Greek, Hebrew and the Gaelic languages of the Celts.

The Normans themselves were originally Vikings, or 'Northmen', who raided, colonised and eventually settled down around the French coastline.

The had sailed up the Seine in their longboats in 900AD under their ferocious leader Rollo and ruled the roost in north eastern France before sailing over to conquer England in 1066 under Duke William of Normandy – better known to posterity as William the Conqueror, or King William I of England.

Granted lands in the newly-conquered England, some of their descendants later acquired territories in Wales, Scotland and Ireland – taking not only their own surnames, but also the practice of adopting a surname, with them.

But it was in England where Norman rule and custom first impacted, particularly in relation to the adoption of surnames.

This is reflected in the famous *Domesday Book*, a massive survey of much of England and Wales, ordered by William I, to determine who owned what, what it was worth and therefore how much they were liable to pay in taxes to the voracious Royal Exchequer.

Completed in 1086 and now held in the National Archives in Kew, London, 'Domesday' was an Old English word meaning 'Day of Judgement.'

This was because, in the words of one contemporary chronicler, "its decisions, like those of the Last Judgement, are unalterable."

It had been a requirement of all those English landholders – from the richest to the poorest – that they identify themselves for the purposes of the survey and for future reference by means of a surname.

This is why the *Domesday Book*, although written in Latin as was the practice for several centuries with both civic and ecclesiastical records, is an invaluable source for the early appearance of a wide range of English surnames.

Several of these names were coined in connection with occupations.

These include Baker and Smith, while Cooks, Chamberlains, Constables and Porters were to be found carrying out duties in large medieval households.

The church's influence can be found in names such as Bishop, Friar and Monk while the popular name of Bennett derives from the late fifth to mid-sixth century Saint Benedict, founder of the Benedictine order of monks.

The early medical profession is represented by Barber, while businessmen produced names that include Merchant and Sellers.

Down at the village watermill, the names that cropped up included Millar/Miller, Walker and Fuller, while other self-explanatory trades included Cooper, Tailor, Mason and Wright.

Even the scenery was utilised as in Moor, Hill, Wood and Forrest – while the hunt and the chase supplied names that include Hunter, Falconer, Fowler and Fox.

Colours are also a source of popular surnames, as in Black, Brown, Gray/Grey, Green and White, and would have denoted the colour of the clothing the person habitually wore or, apart from the obvious exception of 'Green', one's hair colouring or even complexion.

The surname Red developed into Reid, while

Blue was rare and no-one wanted to be associated with yellow.

Rather self-important individuals took surnames that include Goodman and Wiseman, while physical attributes crept into surnames such as Small and Little.

Many families proudly boast the heraldic device known as a Coat of Arms, as featured on our front cover.

The central motif of the Coat of Arms would originally have been what was borne on the shield of a warrior to distinguish himself from others on the battlefield.

Not featured on the Coat of Arms, but highlighted on page three, is the family motto and related crest – with the latter frequently different from the central motif.

Adding further variety to the rich cultural heritage that is represented by surnames is the appearance in recent times in lists of the 100 most common names found in England of ones that include Khan, Patel and Singh – names that have proud roots in the vast sub-continent of India.

Echoes of a far distant past can still be found in our surnames and they can be borne with pride in commemoration of our forebears.

Chapter two:

Ancient roots

Unusual in that it is the source of a number of other wholly separate names that include Hewitt, Howat, Howie, Hutcheson and Hughson, 'Hughes' is ranked 18th in some lists of the 100 most common English surnames.

Popularised as a surname in the wake of the Norman Conquest of 1066, along with many others, it has a number of points of origin.

One is from the Old French personal name 'Hughe', or 'Hue', another from the Germanic 'hugu', meaning 'heart' and from the Celtic ó haodha, indicating 'inspiration', or 'fire'.

The name is also thought to have been popularised through reverence for two saints – St Hugh of Cluny, who lived from 1024 to 1109, and St Hugh of Lincoln, born in 1140 and who died in 1200.

Particularly identified with Wales, with Carmarthenshire recognised as having been one of their early heartlands, one ancient Coat of Arms for a Welsh family of the name gives 'Kymmer yu Edernion' – the name of their lordship – as its motto.

This family, according to some sources, trace a descent from an early tenth century Earl of Hereford who, in turn, was a direct descendant of the semi-mythical Beli Mawr, 'the Great King of Britain.'

The origins and true nature of this fascinating figure are shrouded in mystery.

With Beli Mawr meaning 'Beli the Great', he is recognised as having been the progenitor of what became several of the most powerful royal houses in Wales.

Some sources state the name relates to the Celtic god Belenos, or Belinius, while others assert that 'Beli' stems from the Old Celtic personal name Bolgios, or Belgius.

According to the *Welsh Triads* and other ancient historical sources, he was the father of Caswallawn, or Cassivellaunus, the British chieftain who led resistance to Julius Caesar when he invaded British shores in 54 BC.

Meanwhile, known in Welsh as Cymru, and with the motto of 'Cymru am byth', ('Wales Forever'), this early homeland of those who would come to bear the Hughes name was annexed to the English Crown in 1284.

This boiled over into bloody rebellion in

1294, when Edward I imperiously ordered the conscription to his armed ranks of the famed Welsh longbow men, to help him in his territorial battles with France's Philip IV.

A national leader arose in the form of Madog ap Llywelyn of Merioneth, who inflicted a number of stunning defeats on the English army that had occupied Wales.

But the short-lived rebellion was finally brutally crushed in March of the following year and the nation fully subjugated.

It was not until more than seven hundred years later, in 1998, that the Welsh were granted devolved governing powers through the creation of the National Assembly for Wales, based in Cardiff.

In later centuries bearers of the Hughes name have gained distinction on the battlefield.

Notable among these was Thomas Hughes, a First World War Irish recipient of the Victoria Cross (VC), the highest award for bravery in the face of enemy action for British and Commonwealth forces.

Born in 1885 in Corravoo, Co. Monaghan, he had been a private in the 6th Battalion, The Connaught Rangers, when, in September of 1916 at Guillemont, in France, he returned immediately to the firing line after having his wounds dressed after being injured in an earlier attack.

With his company pinned down by machine-gun fire, he dashed out and, braving the lethal hail of bullets, shot the gunner dead, captured the gun and returned with four prisoners.

Later promoted to the rank of corporal, he died in 1942, while his VC is displayed in the National Army Museum in Chelsea.

The Hughes name has also been particularly prominent in the often cut-throat world of politics, no less so than through William Morris Hughes, the 7th Prime Minister of Australia, who is recognised as having been the longest serving member of the Australian Parliament.

Also recognised as one of the most colourful figures in twentieth century Australian politics, and more popularly known as plain Billy Hughes, he was born in London in 1862 of Welsh parentage.

Immigrating to Australia when he was aged 22, he found itinerant employment as a cook, bush worker and labourer before arriving in Sydney in 1886.

Fourteen years later, the ambitious Hughes had founded and become first president of the powerful Waterside Workers' Union, also finding time to study law and qualify as a barrister.

He first entered the federal Parliament in 1901, as a member of the Labor Party, but would subsequently change his party allegiance five times before his final spell in Parliament from 1944 until his death in 1952 as a Liberal.

It was as a member of the Nationalist Party that he served as 7th Prime Minister of the nation from 1915 to 1923, while his first constituency, one of four different electorates in two different states that he would serve, was Sydney.

Not only the longest serving member of the Parliament, at the time of his death at the age of 90 he was the oldest person ever to have been a member of the Parliament and is the last Australian Prime Minister to be born in Britain.

Thousands of people lined the streets of Sydney on the day of his state funeral, while he was honoured in the form of an Australian postage stamp issued in 1972.

In American politics, Charles Hughes, born in 1862 in Glen Falls, New York was the lawyer and prominent Republican politician who not only served as 36th Governor of New York from 1907 to 1910, but also held high offices such as Secretary of State, from 1921 to 1925, Associate Justice of the Supreme Court from 1910 to 1916 and Chief Justice of the United States from 1930 to 1941.

Also the unsuccessful Republican candidate in the U.S. Presidential election of 1916, he died in 1948.

Bearers of the Hughes name have also distinguished themselves in British politics, with two of the name being raised to the peerage.

Born in 1911 in Dundee, William Hughes was the veteran Labour Party politician who was created a life peer in 1961 as Baron Hughes of Hawkhill, in Dundee, and who died in 1999.

Vice-president, at the time of writing, of the British Humanist Association, Robert Hughes is the former Labour Party politician, born in 1932, who served as MP for Aberdeen North from 1970 to 1997 and as Under Secretary of State for Scotland from 1974 to 1975.

He resigned from the post in protest over the government's Incomes Policy, but was later created Baron Hughes of Woodside, in Aberdeen.

Chapter three:

Invention and enterprise

From battlefields and politics to the very different worlds of enterprise and invention, Howard Robard Hughes, or Howard R. Hughes Sr., was the American lawyer and entrepreneur who revolutionised oil well drilling, making a fortune in the process and laying the foundations of the mighty Hughes business empire that was inherited by his son, Howard R. Hughes Jr.

Born in 1869 in Lancaster, Missouri and later settling in Houston, Texas, Hughes senior practised as a lawyer but turned his attention to the oil business when, in collaboration with Walter Bonona Sharp, he filed the patents for a rock drill bit in 1909.

Known as the Sharp-Hughes Rock Bit, the two-cone rotary device revolutionised the oil industry through its ability to penetrate both medium and hard rock ten times faster than any other drill bit.

He and Sharp further exploited the invention when they formed the Sharp-Hughes Tool Company, with Hughes assuming full ownership following his partner's death in 1912.

Hughes died in 1924, and control of the lucrative business empire passed to his 18-year-old son, Howard R. Hughes Jr., who was destined to become one of the wealthiest, famous and eccentric men in the world.

An industrialist, engineer, aviator and philanthropist, Hughes was also a film producer and director of films such as the 1928 *Two Arabian Knights*, for which he won the first ever Academy Award for Best Director of a Comedy Picture.

Other films include the 1932 *Scarface*, but it was his 1943 film *The Outlaw* that provoked particular controversy at the time.

Starring a rather well-endowed Jane Russell, Hughes put his engineering skills to use in meticulously designing a special brassiere for the actress based on the principles of cantilevered bridge construction.

Recognised as a pioneering aviator, he designed, built and flew the Hughes H-1 Racer and the H-4 Hercules, better known as the *Spruce Goose*, while he also set a number of aviation records.

These included a flight around the world in July of 1938 in what was then the record time of three days and nineteen hours, while a year later he was the recipient of a special Congressional Gold Medal in recognition of having advanced the science of aviation.

Despite his enormous wealth and fame, Hughes became a deeply troubled man, suffering from an obsessive-compulsive disorder that turned him into a virtual recluse during the last ten years of his life.

Living in a series of hotels throughout the United States and around the world and closely guarded by a special body of aides, it was on a flight from Acapulco, in Mexico, to his native Houston that he died in April of 1976.

Kidney failure was given as the cause of death, while he was also found to have been suffering from severe malnutrition.

His legacy survives, however, most notably through the Howard Hughes Medical Institute in Maryland, set up by him in 1953 to pursue biomedical research.

Another particularly enterprising and inventive Hughes was David Hughes, born in London in 1831 and who immigrated to the United States as a young man.

An experimental physicist in the fields of electricity and signalling systems, he fashioned an improved version of a microphone invented earlier by Thomas Edison, and that is why he is recognised today as 'co-inventor of the microphone.'

Other inventions include the induction balance, used in metal detectors, while in 1855, at the age of only 24, he patented The Hughes Telegraph System, which had become an international standard by the time of his death in 1900.

He was awarded a Royal Society Gold Medal in 1885, and the prestigious London-based scientific think-tank also awards an annual Hughes Medal 'in recognition of an original discovery in the physical sciences, particularly electricity or magnetism or their applications.'

From sea captain and sheep farmer to wealthy mine owner and philanthropist, Sir Walter Watson Hughes, born in 1803 in the small Scottish fishing community of Pittenweem, in Fife, is recognised today as "The Father of the University of Adelaide", in South Australia.

Entering the merchant naval service as a young man, he later achieved the rank of captain, undertaking dangerous whaling expeditions to the freezing waters of the Arctic before buying his own ship, *Hero*.

Sailing from the cold of the Arctic to the warmth of the Indian Ocean and the seas of China, he traded opium for a time before buying a sheep farm in the area of Moonta, in South Australia, in 1840.

He had suspected that his land may have been rich in mineral deposits and, accordingly, instructed his shepherds to always be on the lookout for tell-tale signs.

This paid off in 1860 when one of his shepherds, James Boor, discovered what transpired to be deposits of copper. This resulted in Hughes setting up what became the Wheal Hughes copper mine, now a major tourist attraction.

He amassed a fortune, and used £20,000 of this in 1872 to endow what has become the centre of academic excellence known as the University of Adelaide.

Later settling in England, where he bought the estate of Fancourt at Chertsey, in Surrey, he was knighted seven years before his death in 1887.

Another Scot who made a significant contribution to the life of his adopted nation, and one who by coincidence shared the same middle name as Sir Walter, was the composer Robert Watson Hughes.

Born in 1912 in Inverclyde and immigrating

to Melbourne with his family as a child, he later became one of Australia's most distinguished composers, responsible for works that include his magnificent *Symphony No. 1*, and, sixteen years before his death in 2007 at the age of 95, *Song for Exiles*.

The recipient of a number of awards for his services to music, including the 2003 Distinguished Service to Australian Music Award, two years later he received the honour of the Order of Australia.

Also in classical music, Arwell Hughes, born in 1909 near Wrexham, was a leading Welsh orchestral conductor and composer.

Awarded an OBE in 1969 for his services to Welsh music and for his role that same year in organising the Investiture of Charles, Prince of Wales, he died in 1988.

Chapter four:

On the world stage

Best known for her role in *The Liver Birds*, the popular British television comedy series that ran for ten years from 1969, Nerys Hughes is the Welsh actress who was born in Rhyl in 1941.

Her dramatic roles have included the 1984-87 television series *The District Nurse*, for which she won a Variety Club Television Actress of the Year Award.

Across the Atlantic, **Billy Hughes**, born in 1948, was the American actor best known for his roles in a number of television series of the 1960s, including *Lassie*, *Robert Taylor's Detectives*, *The Twilight Zone*, *Dr Kildare* and *Wagon Train*.

Films in which he appeared include the 1961 *Ole Rex*, the 1978 *Convoy* and *I Wish I Was Denny Crane*, released a year after his death in 2005.

In addition to roles in films including the 1974 *The Great Gatsby* and, from 1971, Woody Allen's *Bananas*, **Arthur Hughes** was the American actor of radio, stage and film who was born in Bloomington, Illinois, in 1894 and who died in 1982.

Notable Broadway stage performances of the 1930s included *Mourning Becomes Electra* and *Elizabeth the Queen*, while he also performed on the American radio serials *Just Plain Bill* and *The Fu Manchu Mysteries*.

Another American actor of both stage and film was **Barnard Hughes**, born in 1915 in Bedford Hills, New York, and who died in 2006.

Recipient of a Tony Award in 1978 for Best Actor for his role in the play *Da*, he reprised the role for the 1988 film adaptation, while other films include the 1969 *Midnight Cowboy* and the 1991 *Doc Hollywood*.

Behind the camera lens, **John Wilden Hughes, Jr.**, was the American film director, producer and screenwriter who was born in 1950 in Lansing, Michigan.

Responsible for scripting and directing many successful films of the 1980s and 1990s, including the 1983 *National Lampoon's Vacation*, the 1986 *Ferris Bueller's Day Off* and, from 1990, *Planes, Trains and Automobiles*, he died in 2009.

Winner of a BAFTA (Wales) Award in 1998 for his role in the Welsh language film *Cameleon*, **Aneirin Hughes** is the actor who was born in 1958 in Aberystwyth and whose British television credits include *Spooks*, *Casualty* and *Judge John Deed*.

From film to the highly competitive world of sport, **John Hughes** is the retired Canadian ice hockey defenceman who, during his National Hockey League career, played for the Vancouver Canucks and New York Rangers.

Hughes, who was born in 1954 in Charlottetown, Prince Edward Island, also played in the World Hockey Association for teams that include The Phoenix Roadrunners, Cincinnati Stingers and Indianapolis Racers.

In American football, **Chuck Hughes**, born in 1943 in Philadelphia, was the wide receiver who played in the National Football League (NFL) with the Philadelphia Eagles from 1967 to 1969 and the Detroit Lions from 1970 to 1971.

It was on October 24, 1971, while playing for the Detroit Lions against the Chicago Bears that he suffered a fatal heart attack in the last few minutes of the game – making him, to date, the last NFL player to die on the field during a game.

The Lions, in his honour, 'retired' his player's number of 85 and make an annual award in his name to the team's most improved player.

Bearers of the Hughes name have also displayed great skill on the fields of European football.

Born in 1947 in Barrow-in-Furness, Lancashire, **Emlyn Hughes** was the defender who played for teams that include Blackpool, Liverpool, Rotherham United and Swansea, and who captained the England team for a time in 1974.

The recipient of 62 caps for his country and an inductee of the National Football Museum's Hall of Fame, in Preston, he became a television pundit after his retirement from the game and a panellist on BBC TV's *A Question of Sport*; he died in 2004.

In Scottish football, **John Hughes**, better known by his nickname of "Yogi", derived from the cartoon character Yogi Bear, is the former striker who was born in 1943 in Coatbridge, North Lanarkshire, and who most notably played for Celtic from 1960 until 1971.

It was while he was with Celtic that he was a member of the famous 'Lisbon Lions' squad that won the 1967 European Cup, although he did not play in the final.

A member of the Scotland national team between 1965 and 1970, other teams he played for include the English teams Crystal Palace and

Sunderland, while he also managed Scottish club Stranraer from 1975 to 1976.

His namesake, **John Hughes**, also nicknamed "Yogi", is the former defender who was born in Leith in 1964 and played for clubs that include Falkirk, Celtic and Edinburgh-based club Hibernian; manager of Falkirk from 2002 to 2005, he also managed Hibernian for a time.

Born in 1978 in Wrexham, **Robert Hughes** is the former Welsh defender who played for Aston Villa from 1996 to 1999 and Cardiff City from 2001 to 2003, while **Aaron Hughes** is the Northern Irish footballer who has played for English club Fulham; born in 1979 in Cookstown, he has also captained his national team.

From football to bodybuilding, **Yolanda Hughes**, born in 1963 in Murfreesboro, Tennessee is the professional female bodybuilder who won the heavyweight world Amateur Championship in 1992.

To the sport of angling, one leading nineteenth century authority on the subject was the lawyer **William Hughes**, born in 1803 in Maker, Cornwall, and who died in 1861.

His most notable angling book was his 1842 *The Practical Angler* – decidedly more interesting than his dry and dusty 1833 legal tome *Practical directions for taking instructions for drawing up Wills*.

In the creative world of art, **Arthur Hughes**, born in 1832 in London and who died in 1915, was the English painter and illustrator associated with the Pre-Raphaelite Brotherhood and whose most noted paintings are *The Long Engagement* and *April Love*.

In a different artistic genre, and in contemporary times, **Adam Hughes**, born in 1967 in Riverside, New Jersey is the American comic book artist best known for his cover work on titles that include *Wonder Woman* and *Cat Woman*.

Bearers of the Hughes name have also excelled, and continue to excel, in the creative world of literature.

Holder of the honoured post of British Poet Laureate from 1984 until his death in 1998, **Ted Hughes** was the poet and children's writer born in 1930 in Mytholmroyd, West Yorkshire.

Married from 1956 to the American poet Sylvia Plath until her suicide seven years later, his poetic output includes the 1957 *The Hawk in the Rain*, the 1970 *Crow* and the *Birthday Letters* collection, published in the same year as his death and winner of a T.S. Eliot Prize.

Described as 'the Robert Burns of Wales', **John Ceiriog Hughes**, born in 1832 in Denbighshire and who died in 1887, was the Welsh poet and collector of Welsh folk tunes whose first collection of poetry, *Evening Hours*, was published in 1860.

Born in 1902 in Joplin, Missouri, **James Hughes** was the American poet, novelist and playwright recognised as one of the earliest innovators of 'jazz poetry', and who's most famous work is *The Negro Speaks of Rivers*; he died in 1967.

In the science fiction genre, **Matthew Hughes** is the British-born Canadian writer who also writes crime fiction under the name Matt Hughes.

Born in 1949, his best-selling novels include the 1994 *Fools Errant*, the 1997 *Downshift* and, from 2009, *Hespira*.

Born in 1930 in Alton, Hampshire, **David Hughes** was the English novelist best known for his 1985 *The Pork Butcher* and the 1986 *But for Bunter*; married for a time to the Swedish actress Mai Zetterling, he died in 2005.

Both a crime writer and a literary critic, **Dorothy B. Hughes**, who was born Dorothy Belle Flanagan in 1904 in Kansas City, was an author of popular crime and detective novels.

Her 1943 *The Fallen Sparrow* was adapted for film, as were the 1950 *In a Lonely Place*, starring Humphrey Bogart and her 1947 *Ride the Pink Horse*, starring Robert Montgomery; she died in 1993.

In contemporary times, **Bettany Hughes**, born in London in 1968, is the English historian, writer and broadcaster whose books include the 2005 *Helen of Troy* and whose television documentaries include *Breaking the Seal*, from 2000, and the 2009 *The Roman Invasion of Britain*.

In the equally creative world of music, **John Hughes**, born in 1950, is the Irish musician best known for his management of the Celtic folk and pop band The Corrs, while in rock **Glenn Hughes**, born in Staffordshire in 1952, is the bassist and vocalist who has performed with bands that include Deep Purple, Black Sabbath and Trapeze.

The first white recording artist to have a reggae hit in the reggae homeland of Jamaica, Alexander Minto Hughes, better known as **Judge Dread**, and who died in 1998, also has the rather dubious distinction of having had the most banned songs of all time.

Born in 1945 in the small community of Snodland, in Kent, the English ska and reggae musician's first major hit was the 1972 *Big Six*, while a number of other songs were denied airplay because of their allegedly 'rude' content.

These banned songs are eleven in total, a world record that is duly recorded in the Guinness Book of Records.

From reggae to the genre known as Western Swing, Everett Ishmael Hughes, better known as **Billy Hughes**, was the musician and songwriter born in 1908 in Sallislaw, Oklahoma and whose *Tennessee Saturday Night* became an American No. 1 hit for Red Foley in 1949.

Other songs written by Hughes include the 1953 *I'm Not Looking for an Angel* and, written three years before his death in 1995, *Cheerful Mary in the Rain*.

In the jazz and world music genres, **Brian Hughes**, born in 1955, is the Canadian guitarist whose albums include the 1992 *Under One Sky* and, from 2007, *Live*.

Bearers of the Hughes name have also ventured into the mysterious and often frightening world of the paranormal.

The inspiration for William Peter Blatty's novel *The Exorcist*, later adapted as a cult horror film of the same name, **Father Edward Hughes**, born in 1949, was the Roman Catholic priest of St James Church, in Mt. Rainer, Maryland, who also practised as an exorcist.

It was in 1949 that he was called to Georgetown University Hospital, Washington, to examine a 13-year-old boy thought to have been possessed by demons after using an Ouija board.

As Father Hughes performed his ritual of exorcism, the boy somehow managed to break out of the restraints holding him to his bed and, ripping out a bedspring, viciously attacked him.

He survived the frightening ordeal and returned to St James Church in Mt. Rainer, serving as pastor there until his death in 1980.